Wall Hall Campus
LIBRARY

Hatfield Polytechnic

Wall Hall Campus
Aldenham, Watford
Herts WD2 8AT

This book must be returned or renewed
on or before the last date stamped below.
The library retains the right to recall
books at any time.

Let's visit a
POULTRY FARM

Sarah Doughty
and
Diana Bentley
Reading Consultant
University of Reading

Photographs by
Paul Seheult

Wayland

Let's Visit a Farm

First published in 1989 by
Wayland (Publishers) Ltd
61 Western Road, Hove
East Sussex, BN3 1JD, England

British Library Cataloguing in Publication Data
Doughty, Sarah
  Let's visit a poultry farm.
  1. Livestock: Chickens, —
  For children
  I. Title   II. Bentley, Diana
  III. Series   636.5

  ISBN 1–85210–752–9

Phototypeset by
Kalligraphics Ltd
Horley, Surrey
Printed and bound by
Casterman S.A., Belgium

Contents

All the words that appear
in **bold** are explained in the
glossary on page 28.

This is the poultry farm in Sussex

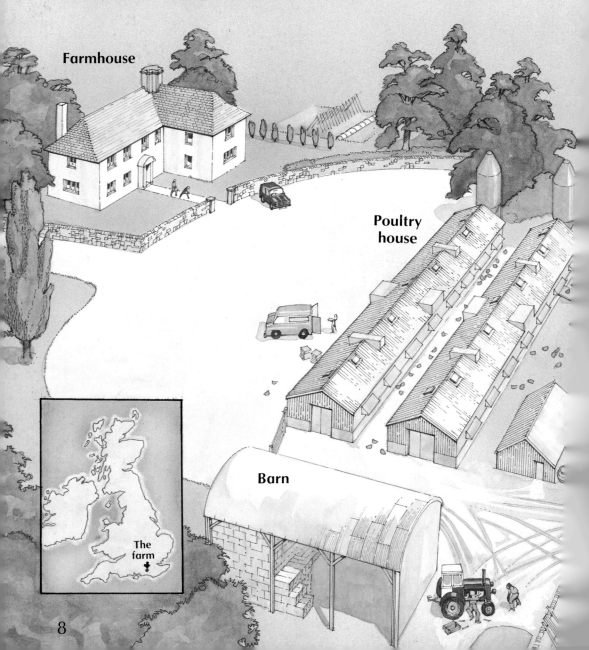

Farmhouse

Poultry
house

Barn

The
farm

8

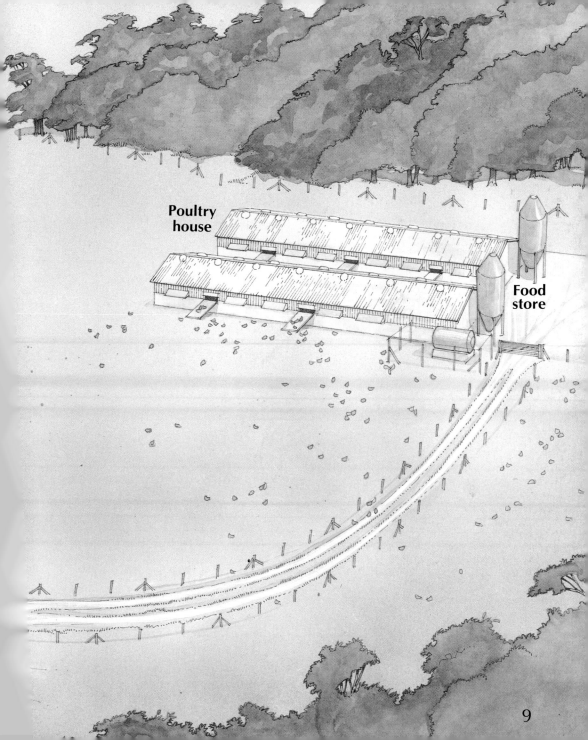

Poultry house

Food store

9

A lorry arrives with the chicks

A lorry arrives at the poultry farm. Inside it is carrying thousands of chicks! These chicks have come from a **hatchery**. The farmer's wife, Mrs Barton, opens the gate to let the lorry enter. All the chicks are carried in crates. They are unloaded from the lorry ready to go into the poultry house.

The chicks go into the poultry house in crates

The farmer, Mr Barton, has prepared the poultry house for the chicks. The house is warm and there is fresh **sawdust** on the floor. The farmer and his wife and helpers are working very hard. They put the crates of chicks on the floor, then tip them all out!

The children come to see the chicks

Here are Lorna and Adam. They like to come and visit
the farm. In the poultry house it is fun to gently pick
up the chicks and feel how soft they are. Some of the
chicks have found water in the little red holders.
Soon they will be fed from the long **feeders**.
Mr Barton wants the chicks to grow quickly in the
eight weeks they spend in the poultry house.

The chicks grow into chickens

Mr Barton is feeding his chicks. They eat a mixture of **grain** from feeders on the floor. The chicks are now a few weeks old. They are losing their soft yellow **down** and are growing new feathers. They will grow to be white chickens. Mr Barton keeps white chickens for their meat. This means when they are fully grown, they will be killed and prepared for sale in the shops.

Mr Barton keeps brown hens for eggs

Here is Mr Barton opening the flap of the poultry house. Inside are his brown **hens**. Mr Barton keeps brown hens for their eggs. He lets his brown hens go outside the poultry house. When hens can do this, it is called **free-range** farming.

The brown hens are outside with the children

The hens follow Lorna and Adam across the field. They like to look for food in the grass. The hens peck at the ground hoping to find a worm or insect to eat.

On many farms the hens are not allowed to go outside. They are kept indoors in cages. Here the hens eat, sleep and lay eggs. This is called **battery** farming.

The brown hens live inside the poultry house

The hens like to come into the poultry house. Here they can eat food from the long feeders. Mr Barton does not need to feed hens himself. A machine sends food along the trough. The hens have a meal eight times a day!

At night the hens **roost** in the nesting-boxes. Mr Barton always makes sure the hens are inside the poultry house at night because of foxes.

The eggs are collected

Every day each hen lays one brown egg. The egg
rolls from the nesting-box into the tray below. The
eggs are collected by the people who work on the
farm. It is dusty and smelly inside the poultry house!
This is why the egg collector wears a mask over
her face.

All the eggs are put into open egg boxes. They are
piled onto a trolley. This trolley of eggs is being
wheeled through the poultry house.

The eggs are sorted into sizes

The eggs are taken to where they are sorted and packed. All the eggs are sorted into different sizes. They are also checked to make sure that only the best eggs are sold to the shops. A lorry comes to collect the eggs and take them to the **packing station**. The eggs will be put into boxes and sold in shops and supermarkets.

Glossary

Battery Where hens live indoors in cages and produce eggs.

Down Soft, fine feathers.

Feeders Long troughs which carry food.

Free-range Poultry that is able to roam freely.

Grain The seed of a cereal such as wheat, barley or maize.

Hatchery A place that produces eggs that have chicks inside. The chicks hatch, or break out of the eggs.

Hens Adult female chickens.

Packing station A place where eggs are packed into boxes and sold to shops.

Roost Hens asleep.

Sawdust Wood-dust, produced when wood is sawn.

Acknowledgement

The publishers would like to thank the farmer and his staff for their help and co-operation in the making of this book.

Books to read

Buildings on the Farm by Peggy Heeks and Ralph
   Whitlock (Wayland, 1984)
On the Farm by Sarah McKenzie (Wayland, 1985)
Poultry on the Farm by Cliff Moon (Wayland, 1983)
Understanding Farm Animals by Ruth Thomson
   (Usborne, 1978)

Places to visit

Notes for parents and teachers

To find out more about visiting a poultry farm, or any other type of farm in
your area, you might like to get in touch with the following organizations:

The Association of Agriculture (Farm Visits Service), Victoria Chambers,
16–29 Strutton Ground, London SW1P 2HP.
They have produced a useful booklet called *Farms to Visit* which gives
details of farms that are open to the public, many with special facilities
for schools.

The National Union of Farmers, Agriculture House, 25–31 Knightsbridge,
London, SW1X 7NJ.
Local branches organize visits to farms. Their addresses can be obtained
from your library.

County Colleges of Agriculture
These exist in most counties. Many have an established Schools Liaison or
Environmental Studies Unit. Contact the Association of Agriculture if you
have difficulty locating your local College of Agriculture.

Index